Poems 2004-2014

Also by Harriet Tarlo

Brancepeth Beck (The Other Press, 1997)
Love/Land (REM Press, 2003)
Poems 1990-2003 (Shearsman Books, 2004)
Nab: Brancepeth Beck, Coast, Nab (etruscan books, 2005)
Sound Unseen, with Judith Tucker (Wild Pansy Press, 2013)
behind land, with Judith Tucker (Wild Pansy Press, 2015)

As Editor
The Ground Aslant: An Anthology of Radical Landscape Poetry
          (Shearsman Books, 2011)

Harriet Tarlo

Poems

2004-2014

Shearsman Books

First published in the United Kingdom in 2015 by
Shearsman Books
50 Westons Hill Drive
Emersons Green
BRISTOL
BS16 7DF

Shearsman Books Ltd Registered Office
30–31 St. James Place, Mangotsfield, Bristol BS16 9JB
(this address not for correspondence)

www.shearsman.com

ISBN 978-1-84861-359-1

ACKNOWLEDGEMENTS
Some of these poems have appeared previously in the following magazines and
journals: *The Capilano Review; Classical Receptions; Ekleksographia; English;
Pilot; Rampike; Yellow Field.*

Also, the following books: An earlier version of 'Particles' in *Clouds Descending*,
Lowry Press, 2008, and individual poems in *Feeling the Pressure: Poetry and
science of climate change*, ed. Paul Munden, British Council, Switzerland,
2008; *Infinite Difference: Other Poetries by U.K. Women Poets*, ed. Carrie Etter,
Shearsman Books, 2010, *The Ground Aslant: An Anthology of Radical Landscape
Poetry*, ed. Harriet Tarlo, Shearsman Books 2011 and *Gathered Here Today:
Celebrating Geraldine Monk at 60*, Newton-le-Willows: The Knives, Forks And
Spoons Press, 2012.

With thanks to all those mentioned in poem dedications and notes and,
especially, to Frances Presley, Scott Thurston and Judith Tucker for their
suggestions at the final editorial stages.

Contents

(I) Relations

(II) Place-time

(III) enviro

(I) Relations

Furry Pod

I haven't got a line at all. Going beyond on the bus. Hermetic unit. Behind the line of not quite clean. Grit connect. Yes, we were on the bus and over the border. Girls Get Life. How to behave in the face of any given situation. Not expecting to be a successful animal. That comes later.

hands on feet

hands on feet / feet on hands
we balance / she pushes forward
into the future with her legs
my feet land / trying not to smash
into the patterned glass door
ornaments / nest of tables
stood below our mother's
mother's portraits ranged
serene / serene / serener even
a smooth face / in her thirties
where we landed

Ben's poem

singing already

robins   blackbirds   finches

the baby's first

lived-in spring

for/tune for/tune for/tune

they sing

it will be

February 2005

Garden (for Laura)

even our roses
shine without care
this year

    feverfew & foxglove
     seedtails pushing
       through loving
         hill to moor
             to garden   grow

     when you come inside from
     the sunshine, it always
     looks dark, little one

     so she leans and learns and leans
                   into light
learning to leave
to come back later

       explore, explore, great explorer
       it's your big world
       though mine is smaller still

seven raspberries left by
blackbirds, bluetits

July 2005

shale and stone and shell

shale and stone and shell is hard
to fall on, aunt's hands under my
shoulder, hauling, pushing me on
sea-salt wing-beat weed – he lifts
it, flaps in my face – will it wrap wetly
round me? Stare at the run of the sea.

That football! Faded it's mine, soft
from the old salty cupboard, want it,
they kick it away. I chase. There's room
to run, but not get lost, uneven over
shale and stone and sand is hard to
fall on, rotting weed, dirty and clean.

1938

i.m. Len Tarlo (1928-2006)

A boy drank milk
        past refreshing
stopping his bike on
        the way back
to Dublin

It wasn't milk, it was
        buttermilk, thinner
but richer too, it was
        his childhood, or that's
how I remembered it

faint

faint full moon at morning
        promise to place   walk
be outside   what the real
       time, light, is
            welling when it comes
            where in the body feels
            like the heart
land tears maybe   flower pigmentations
    inseparable colours, tangled banks
        stalk threads crossing
            not in a stone, grass
            bedded up against it
            roots drawing up
nutrients rising in dreams, he was
      himself, strong clasp, alive
      again, rather never dead
            where in the body, ache
            low in the back
            waiting
only in place words return
      not shorthand recollection
      of coalescence

        once   house
        pram   lane

domestic

2008

it is the people is it warming
the bones of the house soon
to fall into damp decay any
time otherwise snow seeps in
easily or would if you knew how

2009

under finding
their dry goods
small secrete
cupboard under
boot blanket settee
scorning the box
under carrying
the small place
sweet bits quiet

2010

stone workings bones
fall in walls deep
fireplace

2011

each hollowed house
place crease in
          home under
mice spread-creep
          into stone step
          spaces each and
          each to each a
walled windowed
place hollow in
hill fold   sshh

A Spoon for Stein

a curve is a centre if you turn it a round over which
you don't let in substance or do using it using
it in a baby mess throw a curve out of which came
came substance steal a spoon steel it filling
filling the curve is an ending end the handle and
mush the baby out of a stainless mess a stain
is not an object out of a spoon it curves round
around its filling is a centre throw it a spoon
is a missile hit and miss a spoon a mush onto and
of banana rice pear chicken potato apple
again spoon spoony tune let it go throw

near tears

she's up again
        shifting stuff   across, across
        in down up

     shelf sink table worktop

            no go momentum   no slow
                                     pour
            still warm

     stroke head   *careful, careful*   smatter

                        fall
place   set   bowl cup spoon

       hands motion, motion

     put your elbows on the table, girl
     and stop

flush

child sleeping   sweating into
her skin   full length   face down
on her torso   not a baby, a boy
coiling curls salty   spring   his
pores open   voices outside are
nothing   pushing up   his eyes
flick a second   then again
he falls   the last time?

handsome boy 2

       she   stops   wanting
                              to hold still
          a child sweaty
matted hair   wanting them home

        could   it   slow   to
eggbox stuck with a hen a tree pieces of
     chocolate tray a penny

           being re
     aligned   ligaments and muscles into
        new places

               that missing child
      of those years

words don't measure up
against him
if it was

list, listing
is a boat

weights and measures

        unshiftable weight
well-holed
             climb it
      won't slide
and measure, the rhythm
is unlikely
      how much or little
a part until it

      won't slip

mini

she seemed to have shrunk
down mini mouse version
of herself   tiny tight
waist buttons   had loomed
over us   mothers, they
keep re appearing asserting
their deep authority to
bursting   pop! she's gone
                    again

the dust in his study

those particles in the tiny
hairs in your nose
                    tickle

          when it settles slightly
                    smothering
      yet sweet
              and warmth goes
through it settling, scenting
his books   it's there
im pressing his soft – is it still
soft? – flesh   light hairs
      over it   standing up, lying
falling, lying
                    bristling even
they sense me – maybe – a
hovering hand over him

                    take every other
word from this or something
                    and start from there?

creases

chest creases slowly   crossing over, pull
of the gentle breast   first in her big sister   this
slipping, shifting flesh   skin that can be moved
on, a pictogram trail   silver in the sun, wants
tracing or is it drawing?   "no, both" says someone
to their mobile as the girl-crowd gets on   taking
texting the aisle *it's Friday night – come on, come on*
broad back neck of the male flushes, looking at that
skin, look at that   *bare legs in October, wait*
ing on the corner for Kim, hair flaring up with
each passing car electric   she won't give them
the satisfaction, her thick-veined thin hands
folding tight to her bag

mall

At Meadowhall the bags get on / it's a Friday buying for the whole
week thing / packages translucent trapping to rip / diminishing to
less than nothing, they block the aisle / malls over the atlantic / gaudy
spending spaceships settling / a bag, a bag, that luxury label lure / you
your own warm hand against your breast / a beautiful girl sleeping in
public like a princess / her veins outstanding, breeding blood / bright
casual stripe across that growing thing / that link heart, two hearts / a
stripe green pink and white / how the colours go / she likes jewellery / is
passionate about unlikely combinations / her folded bolts of cloth on
open shelving / making, making / thinking quietly about it / a little
daughter picks dandelions: *hold this hold this*

for Tracy Brain, 2008

28

look up

the white lines between
the breasts are the thing
look up look up an invitation
cheeky chappies can do it
hold up – hand over – or lift
it and eat less – reduce your
calorific intake – to do it –
how do they with what
the world gives – reproduce
in to print print print
beige bran brown pink
set in one colour or various
gradations – torso – fade out
gently into your sweet day
reduction pace plan

stay hazy

stay hazy

beech

sing light

robin shift

to rose

tip

greensong

darkening summer
        under-tree, under-cloud
    bramble sweet-flowers
              rain to fall   in the night

in the night
        heart hastens
    out of sleep, weakness
            that was not private

woodland, waiting
        for that torch
    flash, small impressions
            graffiti through poppies
                  in the night

heartbeats go past
        foxgloves don't slow
    them, under bracken
            in July, pushing
pushing up
        in the night, it's their
  month, really
            their time
changing, to change
        completely what we
    see, don't see

never or seldom – talking
        with strangers, her
    face is a changing
            place
    it's the season

small impressions
        going past, both ways
    in the night, waiting
            for a single reader

darkening summer
        all green covers
    all sight, all banks
            drowned down to grey

flat elder clouds
        full ferns, reaching
    up to rain

long time coming
        did you hear her
    answer, how she
            changes heartbeat
                in the night?

here

Being here in August
        sky opened in your
clear eyes un-nameable
        colour against pale
sweep of gathered fields
        heather's depths

Rain fell over you
        through ferns, onto
bracken, your eyes closed
        then wide under
rockledge, hillside, cloudcover
        where swallows fly

white

white went round
you   the weight of you
      woven into white
    each contour of and into
white   which is all colour
      and none known –
paper or cloth – to take
    for taking   letters, lines
              or light
                    lent, lending
      moving over each
white line

graphite

sea-layers sky
        seeing sky   as sea
                 stretched over
    wide sweep   pale skin cliff

           layers   **life**
                         in graphite
           change

surprised by some
      capture
           o pen ed you
                  over-sky   making sure
                       making some strong thing
                  pencil shavings

          falling   each
                 here
                 still

ledge

on the verge

a-verge shaking

                        edge

or waiting wall

            to be wrapped

caught in water   wet

            through

                      waiting to veer

out, to have thrown

           off   averse

ledge

           or not to fall

a one to not   let you lurch

over/into

           pooling water

                not quite fall

re-reading BB

wheel whinge
        bone crack
   and turn
building sound layer
        until gentles
ridiculous and lovely
      all ending up
     on the floor
           playing

   light flickering
    fingers lyric
     of Is
  over strings
       and screens
listening bending
     as much as
          acting

cathedral dream

It was a discourse as well as a place
on the descent of Alette with many
chapels and spaces, little cupboards
and closets in anterooms full of folded
cloths and shoe polishings – I tried and
the black got everywhere. Girls going in
but mostly out of services in unknown
European languages, seeking particular
places with partial maps under high
ceilings, candle and must-scented.
Looking at the back of your neck, your hair,
I realised we'd grown, but there was a
moment when the pinned-on badge had
to be drawn painfully out of the flesh
above the breast, where it had lodged

for Alice Notley, 2013

kin

the beginning of summer / ice cream van down by the reservoir / first bike ride for too many months / toddlers, old folk, wheelchairs out for may bank holiday / it's a relationship between journey and wheels circling / *I've been steady* / *I wouldn't say exactly busy* says the lady

(II) Place-time

```
┌─────────────────┐
│  < SQUARE       │
│       FIELD >   │
└─────────────────┘
```

(i) 14 August 2012, 6.00-7.00am

light pushing up over hill-horizon
    wave-edges within cloud   layer on layer
        light rising, there then gone
              there, now gone
                rosebay pushing up, reflecting pink
      back to circling sky – sun showing now – seconds above
        cloud   *edges of cloud high so light*
         silver-gold, gold-silver
            colours don't have names in clouds
    earth scent warm rising
      in light, nettles, thistles faint
        flowering – profusion & light
            dark arch cloud high above
        now, over cloud, over tinker's hill
      sun rises, clearing capstones,
    catching rosebay heads
green-seed sycamore cluster
        hang
           land softens out, flattens out space
      under light
        last bells of foxglove intense
        red-pink   *cloud lines copying hills*
    mist rising from valley bed

midge pricks, midge pricks

now land shows space

Square Field corner

opens ragwort sepals open up

to be landscape   under sun

blue and blue above

then bright blue white great silver broken

sudden change to smooth pinky grey

dewed land soon to dry

shadow curve of animal path inclines

diagonal across silver field space

each furrow is ridged shadow

bowed farm roof angle delineate

dappling patterned sky, small scudding

out to white and wide against blue

hearing unseen birds in outer air, this balance

of dark and light until – now –

wren hops wall stones

snails cling to stalks

bees begin burr grazing

small heath lands on bramble flower

orange against green morning

it's here

(ii)   15 September 2012, 7.00-8.00am

sun just up
8 swallows shift-balance-shift off
over on 3 cables
spanning lane diagonal
post to cottage, post to cottage, post to cottage
facing all ways, looking
shift-balance all triangles
all angles
not gone yet
but soon
far sun
picks out
playground paint
patched silver-white
stun morning
all thistle, all ragwort
white over walls, wires
never all over
one late thistle
purple in shadow, low to the wall
flowering still
but it will, its will amongst blown
grasses, great plantains, bitten & browning
tall hollowed hogweed
stems, black seeds gone
rising over nab
casting shadows right
to left from field corner
oak and farmhouse sent

long, longer down over

field, impossibly light

running

downdale, catching

every strand, hummock

casting all upstanding

each seedling growing

low in lee of oak

under Autumn wind

single cow stroll, grazing one strip

among many sloping down

parallel walls to low valley

dip, rushy damp

from top field, corner place

near, not quite, square

goose grass falling away

from walls, nettles dry

rustle move low

against stone, magpie follows

magpie over wall onto

elders darkening berry branches

weighting over, taking

what they can

from sun disk

rusted sorrel trails

the eye up

the lane, deep-aged red

of it   and there, that last flash

of last ragwort   & gone

(iii) Square Field from Hullock, 24 Sept. 2012, revised 13 Nov. 2014

from Kay's place across the valley, look over:
it's under the heathered top range, hooking
on and back, on and back, Holme Moss mast
transmitting out, three windmills taking
power up, cutting white strips into moorland
fading blades out into pale-heavy skies
gathering; it's between the grit stone villages
to left and right, above the ridged lines of
weaving sheds, mill tower
diminished   and land is reversed – it was
     only summer and a position taken, as this is,
     a little fold in a green view, a dipping
     or slipping, mined perhaps, lowering to
     an unseen turn behind a triangle of trees,
     woodland fragment echoing orange
     up to tiny bronze oak, green sycamore
     as if aligned across one from
     the other, wind-blown
     markings   but see how, below that diagonal of
                 electric poles, old wooden ones running
                 cables between houses, that particular
                 slant of field under a low stone corner,
                 those slopes sledged down from the
                 farm in winter to darker rushy valley
                 floor are just the same

                 – walls, strips, corners and parallels –
                 years of thinking about dry and damp,
                 sheep and cattle and who owns what

Square Field, Scholes, West Yorkshire

6.30am, 15 Oct 2011

under a near-full moon almost dark up
the path to Inglebrough Caves: water
falling, woodpecker tapping, pheasant
      wings sing down   land

lighten-ing   sheeps' patchy legs
long undocked tails materialise, rabbits
scatter, tall nettle tops   tremble out

up Trow Gill closing in under single
limestone drips full dawn comes
in the face of the hill, the lee of morning
shaded down   distant grass holds
day's sunlight
                suddenly quiet
light wind, fading moon, kestrel slide

Clapham, N. Yorks

Morton Woods

snow on the ground for a week now   seagulls inland low over
cricket pitch looking, looking   east wind out of orange-pink
morning   slipping into woods to wait   water-flow round white
boulders in beck   lines of white along fallen trunks   on each
wide branch   dripping of melt-water, icefalls from close scant
branches   dark holly   as blue streak grows high above   waiting
old bluebell leaves looped frozen in snow   water-flow circles
icicled stone   parts two ways down   meets again under
cutaway ledges where snow has fallen   will fall again into a
different pattern   knowing how to circle and flow

January 2013

AN ENGLISH HOUSE

Bretton Hall, West Yorkshire
2007, revised 2014

(i)

PARCEL OF LAND	CENTRE OF EXCELLENCE	HOSTEL
NURSERY	DAMMED RIVER	KING'S MANOR
BURIAL GROUND	CAMPUS	CAFE
GALLERY	MANOR	DEER SHELTER
HAMLET	OFFICE WING	COLLEGE
SHEEP FOLD	METROPOLITAN DISTRICT COUNCIL	GROUNDS
TRAINING COLLEGE	LAKE	AVENUE OF TREES
ACCOMMODATION	BOTHY	CONSERVATORY
EXTENSION	HIGHER EDUCATION CORPORATION	PARK
PUBLIC OFFICE	LODGE	MANSION
SHOP	OPEN AIR	LIBRARY
HALL	ARTIFICIAL LAKES	REFECTORY
EXHIBITION	PARKING	HISTORIC GARDENS
CAMELLIA HOUSE	THEATRE	STABLE BLOCK
ADMINISTRATION	ESTATE	CHAPEL
TUTORIAL BLOCK	ARCHIVE	PROPERTY

(ii)   Camellia House

circle
North stone face   South glass face
                    hazy blooms in mildew-misted panes

        door creaks in

                                        a certain temperature
iron brackets elevate
                        almost unscented
                                            paths through
                        & under
            humidity

                    contains
                    green shine
            pink white sweetmeats

flower towers   soft falling
for the lady, her exotics   thuds
                                            a rest?   a decay?

        never shatter their shrine
                    grafting and pruning
        keeping it down to scale
                            all we do now is feed 'em

                            beneath, roots wide-creep

(iii)   Mansion

THIS ROOM IS SUITABLE FOR ANY PURPOSE

(iv)   Plaster Relief

wooden shutters in narrow boards floor
un-evening grand mirrors to catch candle
light warm stuff in window dust
biscuits mildew nicks tapestry
hanging eagle fireplace coal
slag neoclassical plaster
work – motif motif motif – grapes
dangle, leaf patterns, Greek
vases doilies below, stucco
above variations on a
theme winning over
the nobility

(v)   In Conference

VISCOUNT
LORD OF THE MANOR
HEAD OF SCHOOL
SIXTY STUDENTS
PRINCIPAL
FIVE SONS AND A DAUGHTER
FIVE HUNDRED STUDENTS
COMMITTEE
MAJOR
LIEUTENANT COLONEL OF HORSE
DIRECTOR OF RESEARCH
TRAINEE TEACHERS
LADY
TWO AND A HALF THOUSAND STUDENTS
MP
MEMBER OF THE ROYAL HOUSEHOLD
WIFE AND DAUGHTER
GENTLEMAN FARMER
DIRECTOR OF LEARNING AND TEACHING
ELDEST SON
SHERIFF OF THE COUNTY
ONE CARETAKER AND A BUCKET

(vi)   Inside Story

High under hills and low over surfaces
following through the last dance
trying to surf it   sweet sanctimony
        of the few remaining
dancing through the furniture
    all that old wood
    not to fossilise   Arabesque! Arabesque!
        over the bookshelves, desks, locking cabinets
    their pretty previous selves
            before the war   after the war
                weight-bearing each other
    pose, pose again   on the sprung wood floor
            suddenly see him, seated,
            quizzical, two years gone
            spying through the sweet
            curled arch of her back   her torso
    flips over alive, alive
in all the sideboards, wing chairs, occasional
            tables, flourish and curlicue   get out, ectoplasmic
                out of the ballroom, the studios   push against
                    the inside air
                        for always

(vii)   Memento

NOTICE   PEN

                                          PEDAL CYCLE

KEY   ART   GRUBBING HOE

              SUGAR SACHET   DISK

      MARE
              MOP   PAPERDOILY

        LAPTOP   HAM KNUCKLEBONE

              MUG   EXOTIC PLANT

FIRE HYDRANT   PRINT

              BOX   DVD

      SHEEP   EGGS

                        INTELLECTUAL PROPERTY
FINE CHINA CUP

                        PROJECT

                                    BOUND BOOK
        NAME PLATE

SMALL CAKE   CAMERA

        DUSTER   BOTTLE OF CHAMPAGNE

(viii)   Away

adrenalin heat   it

slipped into
        her bag   under his cape
                                                riding

        her away
                passing it
                                        on

eat it now, eat it today

                                        warm laugh   a sliver
                                                        of wedding cake

bloodhot flush
                keep it quiet

                                                put it on display

                brazening face

                                                a quick slaughter

                        make it to
                another day

Durham Botanical Gardens

from the path it's all just a scene
different once you're under a tree

the leaf fall, the people spread
circular around trees' shadows
lace version, Japanese collection
some trees female, others male

sound fall circle drop into pool
onto bridge place to sit, making
a hill, settling up, native
and rampant

wilderness exhibit, to stand under
an insect as seeds settle in to mutant
bed, still possible to trip, something
I've learnt from witches' brooms

hut frames up, identifies grass under
leaves, dare touch orange grows brighter
as we near dusk, corkscrew, a natural
looking up, a feel to fall

October 2009

Durham fragment

The thing about driving out not facing being in
under strobe into centre absorbs shops fevered
to go towards and then go back, no go out into
flat land, line villages in grey rain nostalgic but
all different even cathedral tower to aim for

October 2009

A half for Barry

first taste is best, better last
though his was Rimbaud red
       in The Centurion's
            high space
       tiles up to the skylight
       lavatory meets Victoria

down Grainger, Westgate, Side
       bookshop long gone,
municipal planting ragged
       wretched end of summer
blow out, but men still say *hen* and
       help you find your way

dried sick on the high level
       just the bits really
Bigg market's dead yet
       only T.J. Hughes
cheap shoes – but it's five
       and I've to leave for a date
with MacD and mortality

       just keep the lingo

Newcastle Station
September 2009

Particles

CUMBRIAN COAST, 2008

(i) Barrow

    six linked tin sheds
          built on buried dry docks
               high over brick back-to-backs
       as abbey once dwarfed village

                    six linked tin sheds
                    veiling subs' slow sure
                       construction
                    till brief deep launch
                         in lights and flags

      six linked tin sheds block
  Barrow from sea, from Walney, the far side of
      Duddon Sands, from Millom and Haverrig

(ii) Duddon Sands

on the road
the brickworks single chimney
smokes out to sea

black mustard frames
Askam flats
between dune & water
slag pier & limestone outcrop

above
the train slides by
small against the high fells
silent slow along coast

distant, to sea
Midway Island   halfway
up England's shoreline

the slag pier – mussels stringing
off it, slow eroding sea-end, posts
rotting where boats once
moored
kids with their
long lines of want sent into sea
tide   out
mud-sand close-patterning
between tussock pool tussock
each blade's
width and thickness casting
its own shadow into salt pool

low swallow flight
blue dark-shimmers below us
catches wind weight   seems play

ridge stoneware lip
    bowl's edge

                    red lego brick
               each square and circle
                   sea-filled

                                 glass grinding back
                                 to sand

    brick crumbling back
    before its sinter point

                     light switch
                     half-buried

            against mud-sand's
        deep ridge

      lugworms, ragworms burrowing in
          and out of sands
    purifying, making flats through
       particular small changes
             of sediment and water

                         going out for worms or cockles
             you've got to know your gullies and your channels

slow-filling channel
    side-on stealthing

            louder rushing wind
              onshore with and
                behind that yellow
                    sea white stranding
                        edges ripple fast-in

(iii) Outcrops at Haverrig

Black Combe crest
      over ridges   shale spit lines
          pale marram dunes   (their small sea-bright
                    trefoils and succulents)

    between which

          wind-run sand
     settles tiny sandscapes, crumbling angles

           some small shift in

           water or particle, some
           colour   stops it
           into structure

      yet still rushes – dry sea –
    wind-run on
        lying in reach

   settling on letters, making texture
     ridging paper
building falling
falling building

        running this shallow rest
        between spit and dune
        land   and   estuary
        sea   and   Combe

so many small momentary
stayings to fall

(iv) Dunnerholme

before the Norse, before the Scots
        before haematite was found
                close to their shore   what was here?

           at Haverrig
      oyster winkle and mussel
        for the pot
              lichen for dyeing
                    from slow-spread scales
                            on sandstone rock
over the kilns at Dunnerholme
      lime for the land, for building
                clay at Askam

                        through it all, nettles for soup
                        haws for the heart
                        hips for syrup and

        sweet may branches
              for the blessing of the new season

(v) Askam-in-Furness

house corner
thrown to sands
letters in mortar
brick stops flow

RAB

BA   **EHAVEN**

RAD

BRICK
URNES   **LSON**

brick pool   crucible brick, burnt
seawater lighting   again in blast furnace
creosote sheen   wall
back to clay's
melt minerals

RINGT
REDAC

MICKLAM

CRADWELL

FURNESS BRICK
CO LTD
BARROW

(vi) Eskmeals

above highwater mark
　　　below dog-rose, honeysuckle hedgerows
seakale draws on salt and shingle
　　　lumps of pig iron, pebbledash
　and stone　　　its pink-tinged thick-leaved
　　　gray edges glint against small white bloom
　a boot, a bottle, old nets' green/orange tangle
　　　through tall dock stems

heron small-
stepping at pool's edge

　　　　　　razorbill fly by

　　sand rings
　rounded by stone
　　　form a space
to circle
　　　leap into each
round place

　　　　　the range behind us
　　　　　between Seascale and Drigg
　　under Sellafield horizon

they lob things into the sea
and shoot 'em　　　they long range tested out
　　　　　from little letterbox
　　　　　　　shelters

cast old uranium onto
　the sea bed, or is it
　　invisibly over
soft sand dunes, their dry-grained
white wood fragments

                                                    into the air

                                       where skylarks

                              spin around
                              the villages

        shearwaters soar

                     past the turning
                                    radar tower

                                              over to St Bees Head?

(vii) St Bees

down station road
    yellow scales bright-scabbing
        pale limestone walls symbiotic
trail toadflax (ivy-leaved), stonecrop crawls
    over them, valerian and goldenrod
        ribbon-up gaudy summer colour

          England's old diversions:
        priory, cricket field and public school
        golf course (requests appropriate clothing)
        new-shorn sheep grazing, curling up against
        sedge in the field aside a little bridge
        crossing Pow Beck, carving a long ditch
        down to sea

      down station road
   you can walk over the line
      unstaffed   *only stops on request*
stopped station clock   tells no tales
    wooden barrier creaks   cuts off the road
cars stop   3 carriages rumble through   cars go

TRAINS TO CARLISLE		TRAINS TO BARROW

    gatekeepers settle   on bramble and thistle
  vetch, dead nettle, clover corners

round the

      gateposts

   down

Beach Road

                 BEACH   ½ m

      past playground

    chalet park, picnic tables, parking places,

recycling facilities   battered black and white of

     hotel tea rooms, seen better days

       Use of Promenade is
          at your own risk

land forcing up into lumpen head

     guillemots   fly   over

        turning trails

       the groynes

                          swallows

     grab down   float-fly

      pools merge under

        purple light

            sun suppressed behind

dawn

              lit-edge cloud

                 sandstone head

             comes into yellow

      catching the fields in strips

whitening tide's edge

(viii) Harbourside, Workington

cranes' stems hang down over
crates and pipes

shipping in and out of
other countries' stuff

the Derwent flowing quietly
to sea, no mess, no fuss

elder roots in every falling
brick space
corner of the town
thick-flowering, narcotic

(ix) Workington, "Derwent Howe"

over the slag bank top on landscaped paths, through
yellow sloping grass, they walk between harbour mouth
and fenced-off plant, the old furnacemen, teemers,
blowers and loaders, the vesselmen, crane drivers,
straighteners and feeders, the old operators
and their dogs

                         skylarks sing over
                  them, purple cranesbill rich
          all along the bogey road
       to Harrington

kestrel waits – almost still –
    silhouette against cranes

                  you could hear the clang of the rails
                     turning on the cooling banks
                        right through the town

(x) slag bank

years ago, British Steel, they bought from Harrington Pier to
Workington Pier – this was their beach – they could do
anything they wanted, years ago

> slag bank cliff
> strata stops on
> iron finding its
> way down layer
> grey white coal
> ash black

> *the track ran right along the coast –*
> *every six hours the slag engine used t' tip*
> *the furnaces – it used t' light the sky up –*
> *you never seen anything like it, years ago*

> making rails
> – steel out of iron –
> teeming the slag

> so much to send
> on the bogey road
> so much to
> throw on over to

(xi) beach

west-facing, casting fearful
dark, it shadows over
and in to ash white caves
at base   tipped slag
cast stratas to rise up
sculptural

oystercatchers'   sharp
call
fast-falls   high
over
it   all

shaped and lumped by
ladle and trough, lying
as fallen molten moulded
smoothen slabbed down

IRON

waste pocked, its
thick salt-orange pools rust
sea into cups

aside brick, coal, down
grade aggregate

we're collectin' iron – it's just what comes
out the slagbank – that lot in the dump
wagon'll fetch 200 quid or so – it could end up
a car engine block, summat like that

lump hammer lands heavy
over his soft voice
under his blue cap

if you came on to collect scrap years ago
they'd do you for it

from the Firth
brown sea slow sweeps in over
iron-deep sand pushing scum line
through weed on

the workings, handles and bars
stuck crazy out cement blocks, rail
crop ends, brick furnace
corners   stasis
all over

all the mess they've made over the years
they should be made to clean it all up
it'd just be beach then

one gull on her nest
ledge, sticks and twine
as sun rises   straggling down
sand darkens still, only   calling
that white sea line
defines

(xii)

Black Combe spreads wide
shadows over brick houses, stone churches
ghouls of furnaces, turbines wind-spinning under the
Cumbrian hills, their soft-grazing sheep, their tarns and becks
over Sellafield's tall towers and broad reactors, draining cold Wastwater
powering up, cooling down, slow-seeping down to Duddon
out to Irish pasture, Norwegian seas creeping in
over the sands making place, making people
Askam, Ireleth, Millom, Haverrigg
and Dunnerholme

Crossing to Cambridge

Doncaster to Peterborough

seems slow   station signs blurring

fishing by train-lines   even the green looks grey

birds hovering over stubble   sorrel muting

how are the colours of England   revealed

Peterborough to Cambridge

after-image only   narrowly crossing places

Ely just visible through rain   over the fields

almost transparent   with no edges

and dots of colour   made earth below

for Julia Ball
September 2010

Canterbury train

through
water running
sward under
November sun, fen-like
lowland
mist-streaked

**RIVERS WARN YOU
BEFORE THEY FLOOD**

kids on street
at night aloud
energy in rain
bareback knuckles
nodules wet
at cashpoint

**CANTERBURY
SIMPLY INSPIRATIONAL**

wayfarers note
old, pretty stuff
is floodlit,
magic doors
right into it
you have to pay

November 2010

Suspension, Glasgow

trees   lent-a-over
      dwelling   turn
      through night   darker
row row row
frame facing frame
        no dream
      ovals
spindle poplars
d/raining late winter dusk
      dreich as it goes
      landing   hotel hall
humming creak, a crease
      call, city bird
      no mourning

December 2006

London

                                    tube-lit faces
      shaking rocking inwards toes turned to toes
      soothing jiggling baby   red eyes
      individual stillness keeping eyes on out
      not in book   quiet dark platform to feel
      as if you are in fact writing   mandorla

February 2010

The beginning of Birmingham

for Geraldine Monk

CUSTOMERS ARE REQUESTED

fixing a fence

NOT TO FEED THE PIGEONS

curve of a line

ON THE STATION. THEY ARE

not often seen

A NUISANCE AND A POSSIBLE

at times, between

HEALTH HAZARD. PLEASE DO

green – cows under

NOT FEED THE PIGEONS

apple blossom trees

HEALTH HAZARD. PLEASE DO

wide-cornering wings

A NUISANCE AND A POSSIBLE

brown owl landing

ON THE STATION. THEY ARE

yellow light lawn

NOT TO FEED THE PIGEONS

lilac, gorse, laburnum

CUSTOMERS ARE REQUESTED

embankment quilt

June 2012

Totnes Train

suddenly the train's in by the sea
it's a blast, a breeze   DO NOT PUT
YOUR HEAD OUT OF THE WINDOW
Oh, these could be seen as moments
     laces of moments containing
   space   place   time
sand paper next to pink ice cream
in this new notebook – gulls
singing outside 7 Stars Hotel, Totnes
breathing in language, colour like any
other language makes me want to write
into the middle, right into the middle

June 2010

Falmouth, the front

hosing & brushing quayside, dusk's down
deliveries due, all not for naught in warm
southwest winter not quite armistice
in the pub, shimmer window water down
and across *I've got a knife but it's difficult*
to open says old woman in blurred people
carnival open cloud top slice moon to slither

11/11/11

where

where – exactly where – last new year
that man was lost clean over the cliff –
August (nearly) now, sea's last quarter sun
over, the call comes over, a yawn's breath

in fresh fair-lit air – and out again – as the lost
yearn for the wave to pass them over still
summer comes as it will, it will: fleawort
pushing up between crevices, insistent yellow

the couple kiss, full length, their denim legs
folded over each other, a dog's saliva
wets my hand and jacket, licking – all there
in one quick minute – there, exactly there

Trevone, July 2007

triangles and v's

the roofs go up
    slate pyramids and parallelograms
        into village vone

              chimneys low below
                    terrace where London
                people spent summers, swam

                          midwife's old cottage
                  low down Sandy Lane
              right at the bottom
            back to Atlantic

      quiet wind after rough night reveals
fields and doves in morning

        flesh hanging
        clothing that
        worn daily
        comforts small
        sadly
                each patch
                becoming
                responsible with
                age, well

                        here comes the joyous boy
                  aloud into her waking dream

      I hope it clears up a bit and there's some sky

    or a holiday
        years of arbitrary
changes went on

good for rest
or unnerving his
reveries

                            sea journeys
                 cover the pages

                       how land often rises before
          it falls down to coast
                how every object – animal, vegetable, mineral –
                      can be subjected to a series
                           of logical questions
                           that will never come to fruition

Trevone, August 2009

velvet swimming crabs

August high tide   sun
          and moon pulling one against
                                other uncover swept
          sand under ledge
                    four red eyes
                    raised blue pincers
          at the ready
                              quick quick bring the net

                    are you some double creature
                    rearing up fantastical, fierce edge
                    defender *devil crab, witch crab*

                              or two clamped carapaces
                              pincers tangling turning as
                              you're scooped up into
                              the new blue net?

          stripe-bright children running
                    rocky places, expecting action
                    brief possession
                                   can we eat it?, can we eat it?

                              clamped banded round
                              bigger in the bucket
                              sand settling in water

                    better than oystercatcher from above,
                              octopus from below, gripped
                                        by suckers and passed down
                              whole?

          tipped back, they shoot under
                    their ledge much the same
                    or not, we wouldn't know

waiting for the first incoming
wave force into crevice
carapace and on

still clamped and clung in
pre-mating embrace
under the new moon's
strong spring tide

all around
whose rocky shores

Trevone, August 2009

Six Aprils

wind quiet now
dip frost nettle
catch early sun
gulls wings white

rockpools shadow
selves over ice
traceries, weed
down run rock

     3 cormorants look
  out to sea – perfect spacing

oystercatchers' red legs,
beaks against black rock
clack-whistle sounds
like indignance

        shadows cast inland
        first few campion spray
        cloud fly larks above
        sight sing over those
        pounding men

the head, her reticence
the quick of it, sharp of
catchers, flat high sea

      another's writing in my
      not-to-be notes, working out
      which birds waking, wishing
      you held out, holding nerve
      nerves, quick

nail split, splint
feather fragment in front
tick, swallow

force water under
fire ball melt

Trevone 2009-2014

from cabin

14/8/11

      crows struggle with yesterday's pitta
could have given it another tear   instead
they're vulnerable   out in the open   eating
hearts going, ready   to fly any second
into heavy swirl sky   gone now
while I've been writing   that's birds for you

      the children come in anyway
      talking fishes, caves & painting
      as Laurie says, art is long and
      life is breakfast

15/08/11

      tide up to tamarisk   a film cutting at green
a seal that might be there   all under upright
telegraph, wires in sky   how an eye
takes that away   from cabin view

      seeing something where one element
is always moving   dull silver-blue dark swell
      not breaking till   the very unseen edge
pigeon on pole slot into lifeboat house, a dovecote

      flicker white could be gull or spray
the longer it doesn't say (stay)   sight uncertainties
tendency to summations   even aphorisms
    season completes observation   does it?

18/08/11

      angle cliff top turned up
quieter today   flat light   each sun glimmer
a surprise pleasure   *can you set me up?*
      send a postcard   time measure spoon
mother's life management   will not want

20/8/11

    I can't believe we're now on holiday
more of an adventure   fishing line out into sea
without me   still quite calm   sky and water
      stir only slightly   like trying to paint
out of a window   everything else gets in, tide
coming in   "coast" is owned   is it?

21/8/11

      above tamarisk   bursting out of its cut
blue streak pale streak over purply sea
as if watching could prevent disaster   climbing
    to impossible ledges for instance
he closes the window   quiets sea   breaking
    as tide goes out

      high shriek oystercatcher calls
there unseen   land swell over   lying on its
side   up at the hip   down to ragged rock
      white fringes, their lingering pink
schwa   here where you can believe
    yourself to be on the edge of the real
      unsaid   love gone from the life of things

22/8/11

      strange summer mist   it will break through
tidal   water wants rock   we imagine sea
      enjoys edges right up against
this far down land   pushing   islands up
      no flow full on
  for now   post and wire come to the fore
      dark, this grey-white morning

singular

backlit trees frondfall
less how sight changes
what seemed grand, it
shifts – slight shift around
to commonplace or garden
greying graceless away   but
if you are that place, you're
green, great dripping green
after-storm morning
may in Andalucia

2009

morning at Harbour House

between   bays
tall tree   balconies
fishing boat   men in their
orange oilskins go by
one resting   his arm
on the boat   looks out
what sea   does he see?
not-just   pleasure

                 seeker

Whiffin Spit, June 2009

back tide at Whiffin beach

through the silvery
scuttling of purple
shore crabs every
step scattering
over ebbing sea's
trickle back water
eddy about stone

        periwinkles grey-pink surge over
        rockweed, bulbous heads and tubes
        of bull kelp felled and flung up from
        sea forest up-reaching sound
        through sheer numbers
        and between rocks

        grey seals stretch
        at every outcrop
        heads rise – a question

                maples, thick green growth
                down to rock where yellow
                monkey flowers *crowd the damp*
                mossy seeps ... and make a brave
                show said J.E. Underhill in 1919

June 2009

96

Whiffin Spit, *saʔəkʷ*

round the inlet
fir, cedar forest down to water
    shell midden layering, lining coast   12,000 years
                             eating and dying
               sedimental
    [long long time] swash on
    swash littoral drift makes
    spit
               beneath shadowy lit-tipped
       Olympic peaks
Canada geese cross, nuthatches
  call over and forth
    the green spit spine

    wild roses, nodding onions
  humming birds' dark heads buzzing
    in and out of red-orange trumpet glory

          clam shell bowls half
          full of morning sea

    gulls swim behind
fishing boat's
    curve, re-curve
        strewn driftwood on driftwood
   thrown after storm
   settling to rippling
water, wave in
     it's only an inlet
    looking back to the Americas
  or a straddling gate
out to the Pacific   off Mercator map-edge
    the biggest space on the earth

                              stops only at Sakhalin's
               offshore giants piping oil
                                       west to east
     sahaliyan ula angga hada

          pleasure boat   cedar dugout ghost
                  edges silt land's   seeking salmon
                       re-curve, curve   and herring

                              beach peas purple over grey
                                   clam shell beach clatters
                                        thick rim
          otter-debris crack   shore crab
                  speckle purple   scuttle

          ebbing water
                                   back home
                                   I just zoom in on it: Americas:
     Canada: British Columbia: Vancouver Island: Sooke: Whiffin Spit

          a single placing blurs
          as you get closer   digital distance   covers it

June 2009

98

8 Chicago : 2 U.K.

            between times
does it quicken night?
            writing out of time
in NYT margins, clouds
            white on white
peoples' *personal hopes*
            diminishing, diminishing
quick, no duty without
            a notebook or right
to manage a life or marriage
            out of greyish light
river winding dim fields, dark
            houses just sighted
tiny light markers flickering
            rivers widening into
lakes as if pushing land away
            which great lakes, what
names north of Chicago?
            higher and each
flicker is an abundance quelling
            fireflies   pink-lit slice sun
and it's gone, as the screen girl
            tries to shoot, horizon
fades then lights then fades
            again   a long sunset
we fly parallel   water still
            shows pearly, picking up
light, reflecting it back up
            to us, now earth
is dark, sky still blue
            above, deepening cloud
pink soaking away
            all is absorbed

June 2011

mill space, minneapolis

mill space
        rust girders
iron door
        crack craze
window   bent in
        silos where
flow dust fire   swept out
        metal frame
open high onto sky

traffic passing, life that
        displaced this

October 2012

(III) enviro

The Cambrian Explosion

snowballed earth

and the rain falling
outside

evolution occurs by throwing up
variation randomly

the horse and woman
paired by

soft shelly parts
the benefit of having hard parts
we hardly begin to understand

something historical about when

rusting the seas
     iron builds up
        oxygen enters
our atmosphere   on t.v. now
           bright graphics
      strip the layers
    the sensational hole

we can show and show and show

upright

we can see the mammal
distorted by refinement
protruded extruded lips
eyes outlined costs involv
ing imitations of another
animal's fur hair dyed ash
grey-glassed eyes reflect
ing back a pair the same dis
guise as when we stood
upright

Making Work

we are somewhere now

I think
through time

rookery
things that don't go
away
often landscapes and people
on the same page –
the sea breached the
shingle beach defences
manage to grab
that light
the shipwrecked visitor's
experience
around the edge
of deep England
the idea is mine

the sea has got no identity
really

bodies in conference

warm shifts room from cool / bodies defeating air
conditioning / lure in her conference limbs crossing over
each other / knee imprinting calf / a rest but also an
energy / elbow on the other arm on top of hand

creased shirts of men / light reflects words on shirts as he
weaves them / arms sprawling among them / blood
rising mottled in the neck of the performer / hand moving
down his body protectively

why can't we just get up and move around?
asks Richard

for Richard Kerridge

outside orangery

pond through
      steps on
branches or
      reeds

moorhen head
      pushing each
stroke forward
      and round

leaf crust
      layer under
frost

bullfinch white
      streak catches
cold sunlight

ice like scum

      what do you have
to do   what's next
      got to see
got to see

      politics behind
the door
      oh
there she is

      valentine
do you
      matter

      laughing   will
they know
      how to do it right

are there buds yet?

four panels

grass	stone	brick	earthenware
planted	away	expect	lane
selected	afternoon	beaten	seems
choice	late	bricket	day

late selected day   our expectations, any

bricket beaten seems   way day down

too afternoon   full   valerian lane, lurid red

earthenware   staked   her short walk

in a jar   journey round and

                   round the garden

not another brief

unpunctuated lyric, hinting

not planting any earthen

ware   grass   stone   brick

          four panels of a timberframe

          and again

          apply for everything

synapses

at a snap   short circuit

light the mind   lift

      this time of year

we might

         take her leaves

    (six months lying)

stick em in a bin bag

    lighter mind lined

out of a drawer

flashfire

it's up

    tealight in a pumpkin

dusk shreds, strips sky

line behind night branches

beyond blue-grey into bruise

purple too much touch

spreads pink last light

over trees, over dim green

brink

honeysuckle

honeysuckle can throw
shoots up, bearing
its own weight
into air

if there's nothing
to clamber
up

Lunaria

i.m. Ric Caddel 1949-2003

old-fashioned honesty
wasted in a dark corner
by the compost – each
purple petal drying into

pearly pods ladies wanted
for their church arrangements
cruciferous transparency
dishonest dollars easily sown

left alone, in flower, it's a
four-petalled structure
so simple, you don't have
to think of it any longer

Ryecroft, May 2013

beeches

-yellow-copper-gold-not-money-but-silas-glint-paper-
shape-wrinkle-cloth-lying-not-flat-fallen-close-
of-autumn-into winter-copper-yellow-gold- still-
hanging-even-bronze-not-like-money-or moon-glint-
in-morning-in-grey-morning-against-blue-white-sky-
early-winter-falling-gold-copper-yellow-bronze-even-green
holding-holding-on-flat-against-watery-sky-against-
grey-blue-white-over-fallen-into-darker-shadow-
earth-mud-bracken-making-autumn-ground-mulching-into
winter-into earth-tentacular-roots-of-gold-bronze-
copper-not-like-money-making-their-own-not
like-breeding-just-touching-under-trees-each-leaf
holds-and-falls-holds-and-falls-touches itself-
each-others-copper-yellow-gold-bronze-even-green-
all-seasons-in-november-from bare-to-green-bronze-to
gone-float-to-mulch-in-every-change-white-blue-grey-
to-falling-rain-feeding-falling-feeding-falling-in-
night-wind-stir-storm-sounds-sounding-like
sea-tide-sounds-like-winter-coming-in-

acquisition

having an interest in
>gain
>>unplanned

they happen anyway
all those long Latinate words

>>building a super
>structure
>shoes, letter-racks,
>buckets and spades

slip of a celcius away

grains

grain caverns castles slipping channels
trenches slide fortifications slow capsize:
are you alive, you many small fallings?
Abandon your barriers for inside England –
don't come back to look for stuff, beach comber.
It's all under the flood: coffee cup castles, single
shoes, the gaudy towels of our dead parents,
sea crashing on rocks, as per memory

M62 East

last evening, driving down
to Delf, twirling round the
hills & dales of Halifax &
Huddersfield, Saddleworth
& Rotherham, M62 beneath:
it's just a powerful snake
stand against green April up
opening those shapes and
the dark cracks between
which we guilty slip
always seen, always seen
under the sky-bright sun's
everlasting perspective
run away home, metal
baby, run away home

summer solstice, manchester, uk 2007

"Water flooded the school, the maize mill and all the houses and the entire village took refuge in church. My house and 15 chickens were washed away. Afterwards, I relocated to a neighbouring village where I constructed a temporary shelter using reed"
(Chipika Kalemba, 84)

we haven't had rain
we've had too much rain

in heavy june rain they wait under horse chestnuts wide wings as crawls slow wheel past headlights to exhaust headlights to exhaust headlights exhaust light head light exhaust cramming round about about round water running the other way down side gutter pavement she took turns for the sake of it Stockport Wilmslow Macclesfield Alderley Edge enter exit enter exit clotted clammed up city tuck straight up **children please drive slowly** not easy to hold the road packed up stay clam calm town on town on town slowing slow down the hospital the shining park light june

we haven't had rain
we've had too much rain

and there's a birth we learn to be born she came out calm her head was just the right shape this time and they took their responsibility seriously right away easy easy in the west world way swung her home from the unit through green grey fields past cowshat campsite under heavy june rain no sweat no sway we just do did it all our own sweet selves way

we haven't had rain
we've had too much rain

shelter temporary shelter impermeable to water under layer on layer of polyester polyurethane neoprene flame retardant PVC stretched out stretched out stretch out fine for a night on my high rise power plug airbed **please leave the amenities clean and have a good time!** coming home from camping after sweatheavy early hours night showering steam in the morning washing it all away washing it all away

> *we haven't had rain*
> *we've had too much rain*

cut off the motorway try to stay clam calm think of the may june elderflowers clotting trees down season summer curving round away from to home purple points pink digitalis digitalis oncoming oncoming oncoming bumping over the peaks light pasture dark leaf cream clustering pollen dust swirls the gutter

Friday Piece

Responsibility is the ability to respond (Robert Duncan)

Convolvulaceae: Members of the family are well known as showy garden
plants (e.g. morning glory) and as troublesome weeds (e.g. bindweed)
(Wikipedia)

Come on children, it's tidy up time, tidy up time, tidy up time
(Playgroup teacher)

morning glory tender
morning climbing into
autumn falling beyond
her season winding and
 clasping where she can
up up to her spectacular
sun

Sheffield after the flood:
bindweed straggling over
the post and railing
mud silted the street
barriers fell at the
football ground

apply the canary test: it soon tells you when
it's too late.   start with the coral reef
the canary in the global coal mine
a fine metaphor with a grand historical heritage

CREATE CREATE CREATE A CARBON MARKET!
A BRAND NEW CAPITALIST ENTERPRISE

waiting for the morning train
frost on the oakleaves quiet
bindweed falling to frost
at last   on the station
autumn   waiting to go

*Each Autumn, thousands of tonnes of
leaves fall on the   railway line*

*A mature lineside tree has between 10,000
and 50,000 leaves*

waiting to stop momentum

*Thousands of tonnes of leaves fall onto
railway lines each year*

child's wail cuts through
suburban garden fences sep
aration/separation/separation

*There are 21,000 miles of track to keep
clear*

one on one on one

*The cost of lineside vegetation manage-
ment (pruning and felling) of trees is
between £20,000 and £50,000 per mile*

flaw
facing every which way

*Autumn costs the rail industry approx-
imately £50 million per year including:
£10 million for vegetation management,
£25m for autumn train borne operations,
£5m for 'hot spot' teams and other staff
/operational costs, £10m for damage to
trains and track from leaf fall.*

TRYING TO DISCRIMINATE, DISCRIMINATE, DON'T SYSTEMISE
DON'T CENTRALISE, LEARN TO MAKE THINGS DISAPPEAR
WE CAN SIMPLIFY OUR LIVES!

The River Don churns mud up
tree trunks, branches weighed
down into the water

> we long thin lit rush through
> it all our little round spotlights
> gleaming over the june dim
> windows lit windows lit windows
> lit windows gleaming electric

> > under black cloud banks
> > still down-dropping

> purple buddleia, the butterfly plant
> bursts between torn up tracks
> excavated sites, trees grabbed down from steep steep
> banks and slopes as the
> cranes crawl beside, building, building
> *desirable riverside residences*

CAPITALISE! CAPITALISE!
DON'T FORGET TO ADVERTISE!

mortgage was no longer possible · it depended too much on
the future · it was suggested that the house, our only security,
consumed too much energy · we needed to start from scratch ·
originally (the 1600s they thought) it had been a two room affair,
cows at the bottom, people on the top · then a farmhouse, four
square stone rooms with thick arched doorways and a well · by
the 1800s another storey had been added for weaving, cottage
industry they called it, thirteen small windows stretching from
one side to the other, facing the morning sun · in the 1970s

some middle class family built a generous extension on one
end · now that really was unnecessary, far too much glass, only
there for the view · we could start with that, bring it down,
keep peeling back

> to which point, the byrehouse again?
> the nourishment, warmth, meat
> and comradeship of the family cows

> they'd forgotten it, if it ever was

so glad we went to Spain this year
to see the sun shining in its morning
glory through the bougainvillea
get away from all this rain

> they are all buying in
> *aglee, aglow* with
> approbation from
> above *aglow aglee*
> with bright blue shiny
> swimming pools a fine
> ride time away on a jet
> airplane riding high
> through the atmosphere
> shooting lines through
> the pale pale sky

> > getting away, getting away from
> > the robin
> > the school yard gate
> > the light-responsive office
> > the September cobwebs
> > the house
> > the calendar
> > the ripening apples
> > the mother on the phone
> > the washing

123

                                    the season, the people,
                                        the hills coming
                                    and going under
                                        the weather
                                            life
                                             as
                                             it
                                          goes on
                                           living
               the unexamined life is not worth living

the house, of solid Yorkshire stone, became a diminished
version of itself · no, it wasn't the house at all, it was a small flat
or office, artificially lit, in a tall tower · very little space for the
children · the solid stone house with magical rooms was never
ours or it was and someone – they – had the power to take it
away · no, it was still there but transformed · all the small
rooms, orange and blue and purple, had become big public
spaces with bright square white lights set in to their ceilings
· it would not go back · the smell of stone had turned to the
metallic scent of coinage · all that money we had poured into
the house, a barricade, had come to the surface, plastering the
shiny public walls of the tower · it was a certainty that in the
future the whole thing would fall, like all the others

                              (can that individual simplify
                              her inherited life?   I
                              not I   I   not I
                              fellowship not family, pulling it
                                        all back in)

        re turning   the need of sleep
        long pull down   recovery
        a sweet-full fall   if you let it so
        often it isn't   there's those
        habitual expectations of the daily
        sweeping, pushing   the brush back

against something hard   dried on
trying to regain   *that clear caressive sight*
                              convolvulus
                              crept out into a wasteground
                              world to be
                              not to be
                              responsible for
                              living

WE EXPECT IT TO CONTINUE
THE ARCTIC – THE LAST FRONTIER!

flags under the sea ice
cut length, breadth, width, *license*
my roving hands to slice the cake
every which way and eat slow
warming ice, a baked Alaska

> *"This isn't the fifteenth century," Canadian Foreign Minister*
> *Peter MacKay told the CTV channel*

        rush down under the ice ledges
        the melting shelf as it slides into
        a fish-threaded sea

> *It was so lovely down there. The yellowish ground is around*
> *us, no sea dwellers are seen, said Artur Chilingarov*

Circling as it falls, Russia Canada Am-
erica Norway Denmark, waiting, marking
territory – *this isn't the 15th Century* –
oil   gas minerals wait under the ice
deep in whose sweet continental ledge
send in the scientists, send in the military
send in the ice-breakers

GLOBALITY! THE WORLD WILL BECOME ITS OWN EMPIRE
RICHES GALORE EVEN MORE SHALL BE OURS

I look forward very much to seeing this
effort to perform or accomplish something, attempt
this trial of the future

Being on the two-bit train
          where it crosses the M1, first motorway in Britain, 'sixties
          dream of fast flow green on blue on red on silver stuck fast,
          slow move, stuck fast, slow move rush hour below

                    where wild roses & graffiti sprawl the wall
                    roof triangles of the back-to-backs push
                    on to Barnsley Junction, the old world
                    jagger judders on, two carriages over
                    the viaducts, casting its toy shadow
                    on Penistone's green sward scrub

                                        and we can see ourselves
                              scorning steel and glass, five speeds and
                              climate control as we rattle
                              over the tops

     thru the tunnel, sound builds
     into emergency no end stop
     to this moment momentum
     tree train tunnel thru ferns lens
     up thru leaves we look or ditto
     down banks fall away vertig-
     inous scape shift attempting
     straight course thru hilly
     terrain all over England tin
     baths enamel sinks our dom-
     estic detritus out of which
     cows drink under plastic tatter
     flags thru tree tunnel leaves

to the close walled city, the Don
her river (which) city slice roof tiles
cranes, brick banks of windows
channelled by ex-industries, into
the new millennial zone, bright
interchange on our old rolling
stock   who wants it?

Please do not leave luggage unattended
For your safety and comfort
Security Personnel tour this station 24 hours a day

suck, suck like a toddler on your
sweet plastic teat, nonspillage   *[Caution: hot liquid]*
Safety Security Comfort
terror terror terror

            outside the station
            50 mill spent on this
            millennial silver space

                    civic fountain plays water
                    energy water a recirc
                    ulating system bringing *natural energy* into the
                    city
                            silver stiletto spiking along paving
                            wet walls shadows moving within
                            them, getting faster all the time

            machine thrub pumping
            behind it all spring fall
            speed separation from
            October water   with no leaves floating

    COME INTO THE PAST TO FIND THE FUTURE!
    YOU CAN CHANGE THE ENDING THIS TIME

where things were stone
steel cuts fine bold
perforations; metal seats
made in Warrington, city
litter bins, rail-guards
and
art: a wall of steel reflects
the skin does not give
behind crowd control

COME OUT, COME OUT
COME OUT OF YOUR WALL
SEE PAST STEEL OUT OF
NOWHERE

*He went out of the station, still discontented and unhappy, muttering
"If I could but see it! if I could but see it!"*

*Multipurpose vehicles (MPVs) are fitted with lasers to blast leaf mulch off
the track and apply a sand based gel called 'Sandite' to the rails*

*The icebreaker uses great momentum and power to drive its bow up onto the
ice, breaking the ice under the immense weight of the ship*

mass times velocity is the fundamental force of motion

waiting to stop momentum
it careers downwards under the steep bank

deciduous, composting stocks
moor cutting turf
clean off

insurmountable chasm

(i)

found words	over	space list
shunting sound	leaf	dust under
learning to	hesitate	leave it
long and longer		over-creepage
	ivy	

(ii)

scabbed apples, small pears
leeks sweet folded greens
dark to light, light to dark
hidden beet purples
white potatoes, stone
bent in autumn earth

(iii)

there are rocks

rich loam   broken

                                sun ⟵——— baked

                                              crumbled

          oak-leaves

          grass reeds

          dusty herbs

          vine-leaves

                    withered berries

                    actual bodily death

                              black earth, passionate things

                                        of earth

against which

          red and rust-colour

                    black-purple   dank lips, clustering

                              locks, burnt crisp

          and, beyond exuberance, inevitable decay

                    life, old forms in

                    new environments

                    Theocritus

(iv)

offered objects

his rabbit-stick, his bright axe,
his plane and his revolving
auger, his hide, his well-cut
crook, his curdling buckets,
his pipes, his honeyed gifts

(v)

This is the one   with which
                    I most identify   developed over such
a long period, I no longer remember
                    the influences   a long period of struggling   to get
        sourdough right   at a time   when information was not
                    easy   was contradictory
                                        when you found it
        This dough
                    a mixture of white and wholemeal flours
            is very gentle and forgiving

(vi)

Rose, harsh rose
reed, slashed and torn
marked with rich grain
the white violet
root tangled in sand

(vii)

stream is trampled
        heel   ...   cut deep
    show dark purple
            dead leaf-spine
        root snapped
                clutched larch
bent back   ...   clear
        no trace

(viii)

waiting necessity

why not let

the pears cling

protected

to the empty

branch   ripen of themselves

                         re-write themselves

beauty without strength

chokes out life

~~in some~~ terrible

~~wind-tortured~~ place

(ix)

another life holds what this lacks

unmoving, quiet

dissatisfaction

madness upon madness

to crowd   posed against   movement of

(to) crowd

no garden beyond

(x)

weight

crashcrack greencrushed

swirlhurled sinkstone

(xi)

landcut

sunder	struck lost face
your space	ellipsis land
glass-ground	blue-green
sea	grey grace
literal liminal	in pattern
drawing	**loss**
place	gets stuck

Notes

P11 'Furry Pod': the title comes from Maurice Scully's *Livelihood* set of books.

P37 'Re-reading BB': that is, Basil Bunting; "ridiculous and lovely" is from *Briggflatts*.

P43 'Square Field', 14 August 2012, 6.00-7.00am: italicised text from texts sent on the same morning from Judith Tucker watching the sun rise a valley away.

P60 'A half for Barry': Barry is Barry MacSweeney; MacD, Hugh MacDiarmid.

P50 'AN ENGLISH HOUSE': some of these poems appear in *Pilot: A Journal of Contemporary Poetry* (2007), SUNY, Buffalo, NY, U.S.A. and *Infinite Difference: Other Poetries by U.K. Women Poets*, ed. Carrie Etter, Shearsman Books, 2010.

P61 'Particles' was written from an invitation to collaborate with Jem Southam and very short texts from it appeared on the wall with his *Clouds Descending* exhibitions at the Lowry, Salford Quays, 2008 and Tullie House, Cumbria, 2009. An earlier version of the full text appears in *Clouds Descending*, Lowry Press, 2008.

P81 'The beginning of Birmingham' was requested by Scott Thurston for *Gathered Here Today: Celebrating Geraldine Monk at 60*, Newton-le-Willows: The Knives, Forks And Spoons Press, 2012.

P91 'from cabin': Laurie is Laurie Duggan and the quotation from *Crab and Winkle*, Shearsman Books, 2009.

P106 'Making Work' is entirely composed of words spoken by delegates to the Land, Water and the Visual Arts Conference, Plymouth 2007.

P108 'bodies in conference' was written at the Poetic Ecologies Conference, Université Libre de Bruxelles, 14-17 May 2008.

P116 "grains": "are you alive?" is from H.D.'s 'The Pool'

P118 'summer solstice, manchester, uk 2007' was commissioned for *Feeling the Pressure: Poetry and science of Climate Change*, ed. Paul Mun-

(viii)

waiting necessity

why not let

the pears cling

protected

to the empty

branch   ripen of themselves

re-write themselves

beauty without strength

chokes out life

~~in some~~ terrible

~~wind-tortured~~ place

(ix)

another life holds what this lacks

unmoving, quiet

dissatisfaction

madness upon madness

to crowd   posed against   movement of

(to) crowd

no garden beyond

(x)

weight
crashcrack greencrushed
swirlhurled sinkstone

(xi)

landcut

sunder	struck lost face
your space	ellipsis land
glass-ground	blue-green
sea	grey grace
literal liminal	in pattern
drawing	**loss**
place	gets stuck

den, British Council, Switzerland, 2008. Thanks to Kate Nustedt who quoted Malawi villagers as saying "We haven't had rain. We've had too much rain" and suggested I read "Climate change and smallholder farmers in Malawi: Understanding poor people's experiences in climate change adaptation (A Report by ActionAid, October 2006)" from which Chipika Kalemba's quote came.

P120 'Friday Piece' appears in an earlier form in *Rampike* 18/1, Special Issue on Eco-poetics. In June 2007 the city of Sheffield in Yorkshire, England, experienced bad flooding. Italicised quotations are attributable to Network Rail website, "Dealing with the Weather"; Lorine Niedecker; Socrates; Kathleen Fraser; Denise Levertov; Oxford English Dictionary definition of "essay"; BBC News website; William Morris, *News from Nowhere* and Descartes.

P129 "insurmountable chasm": these poems were originally embedded in an essay entitled "'An Insurmountable Chasm?'": Re-visiting, Re-imagining and Re-writing Classical Pastoral through the Modernist Poetry of H.D.', *Classical Receptions*, Nov. 2012. Thanks to the editor, Fiona Cox, for suggesting I wrote it. Poems (iii), (vi), (vii), (viii), (ix) and (x) are all composed from the texts of H.D., being 'Curled Thyme' (an essay on Theocritus); the *Sea Garden* poems; 'Pursuit'; 'Sheltered Garden'; 'The Gift' and 'The Storm'. Poem (iv) is from Peter Jay's translations of Leonidas of Tarentum's epigrams in Peter Jay, (ed), *The Greek Anthology and Other Ancient Epigrams* (Harmondsworth, Middlesex: Penguin, 1973). Poem (v) is from Mick Hartley's *Sourdough Made Simple: Techniques and Recipes from Bethesda Bakers* (Bethesda: The Partisan Press, 2010). The rest are "original".

Lightning Source UK Ltd.
Milton Keynes UK
UKOW04f0629071015

259965UK00002B/78/P